Clarke Elementary School

567.9
Demi.   Find Demi's dinosaurs : an animal game book.

T 302375

Gift of the Clarke School
Book Fund 2/90

P9-DCB-451

SWAMPSCOTT ELEMENTARY SCHOOL LIBRARIES
SWAMPSCOTT, MASSACHUSETTS

**A CLARKE SCHOOL
BOOK FUND
BOOK**

Thanks to the following families
for participating in the
Clarke School Book Fund:

REED

The Clarke School Staff received
this thoughtfulness from
Jessica & Tom Reed

FIND DEMI'S DINOSAURS

SWAMPSCOTT ELEMENTARY SCHOOL LIBRARIES
SWAMPSCOTT, MASSACHUSETTS

PROTOCERATOPS

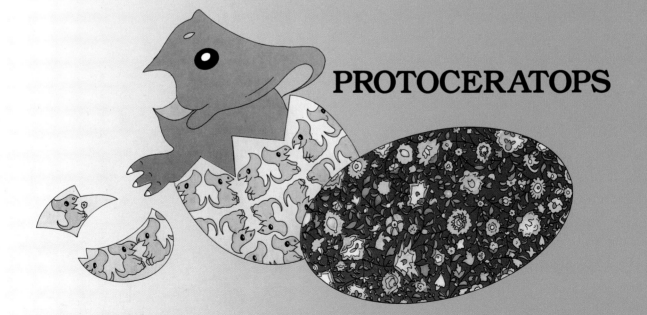

FIND DEMI'S DINOSAURS

An Animal Game Book

Grosset & Dunlap · New York

Copyright © 1989 by Demi. All rights reserved. Published by Grosset &
Dunlap, Inc., a member of The Putnam Publishing Group, New York. Published
simultaneously in Canada. Printed in Singapore. Library of Congress Catalog
Card Number: 88-82977 ISBN 0-448-19020-6   A B C D E F G H I J

BRACHIOSAURUS

Can you fi...
BRACHIOSA...

Can you fi...
RHAMPHORHY...

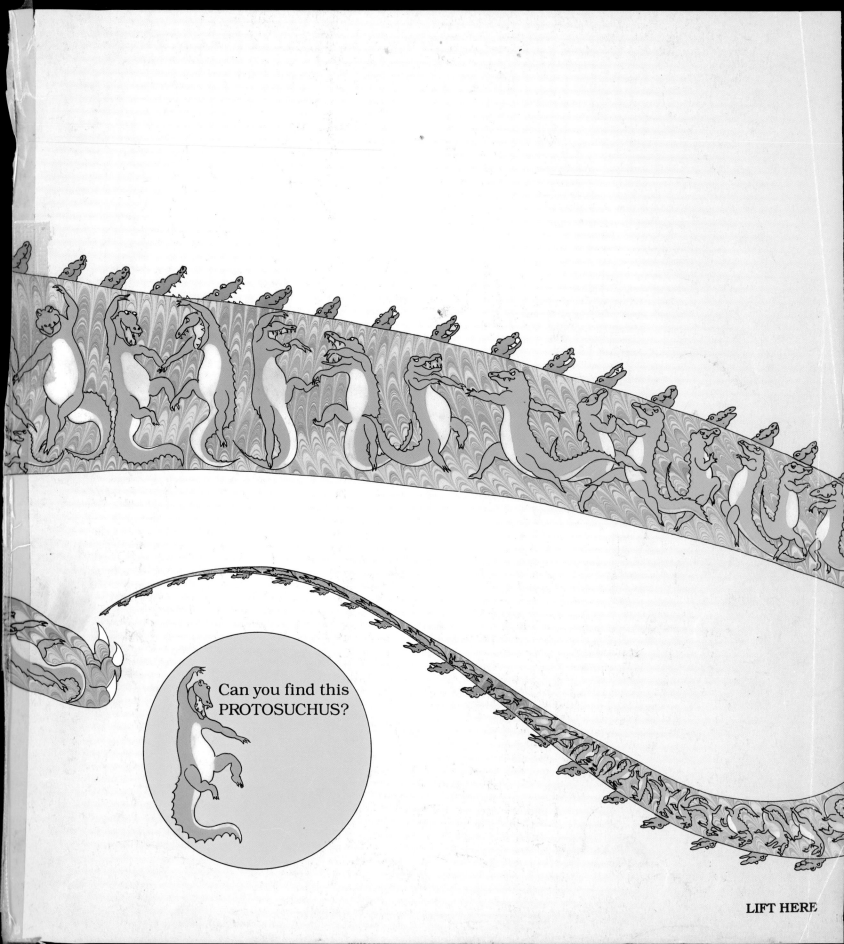

Can you find this PROTOSUCHUS?

LIFT HERE

PROTOSUCHUS

For Lucy Lockwood Hitz
who drew this dinosaur

THERE'S MORE TO THIS PAGE ➡

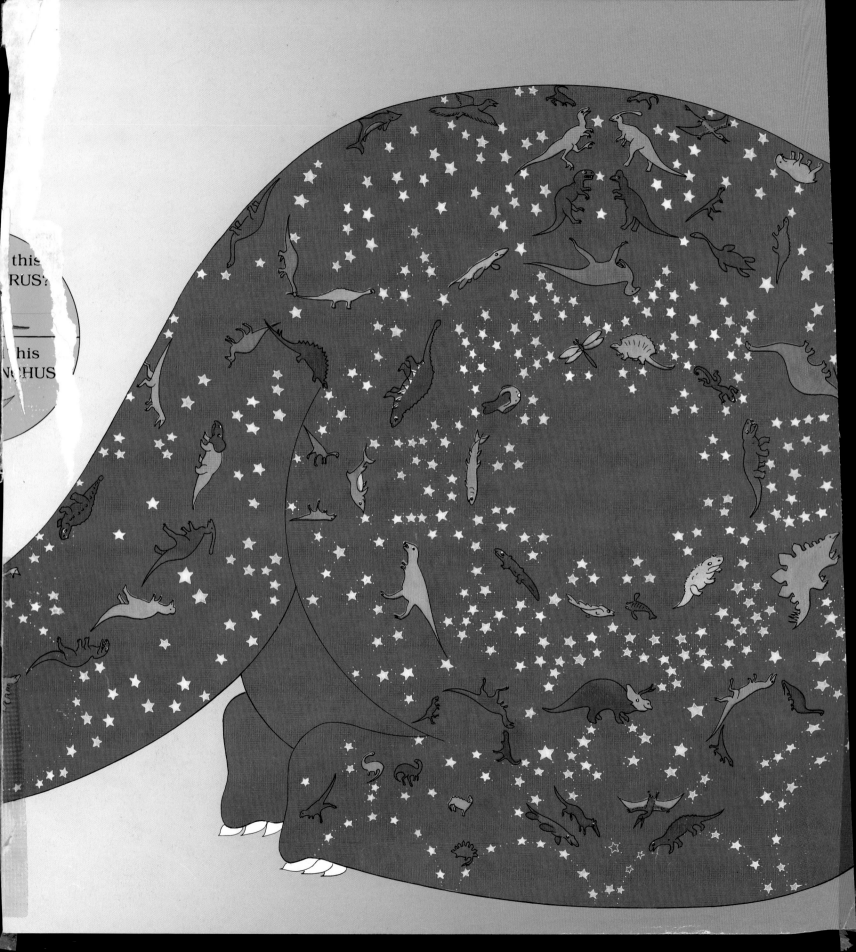

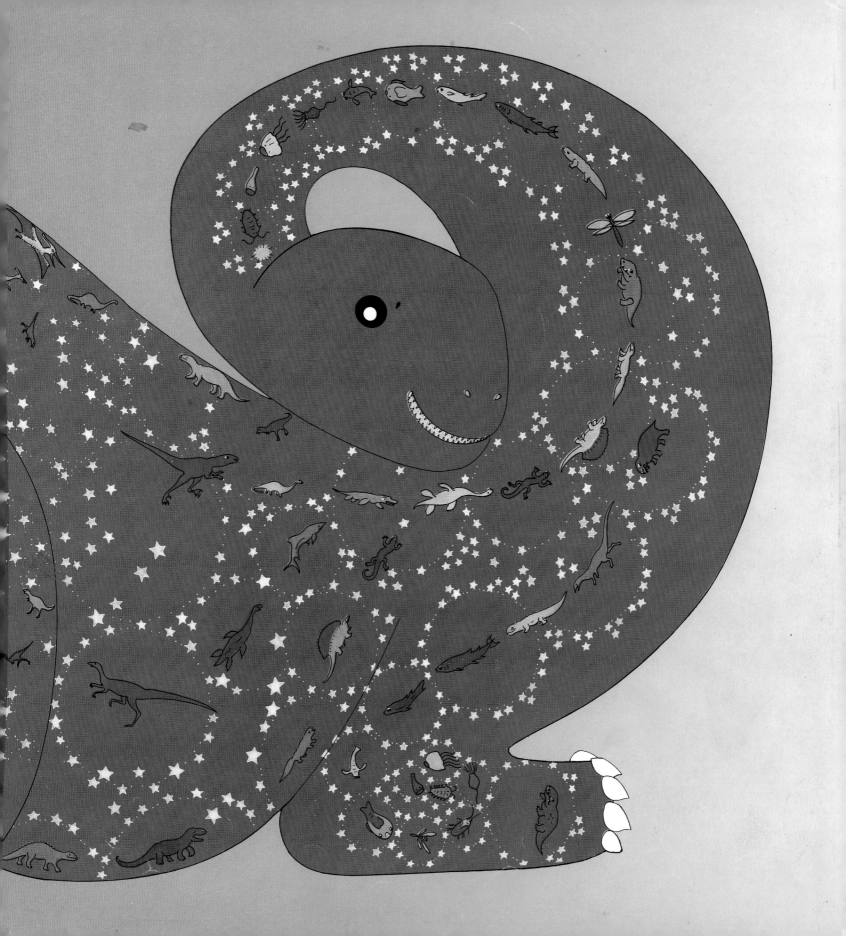

STEGOSAURUS BABY

Can you find this
STEGOSAURUS?

Can you find this
TYRANNOSAURUS?

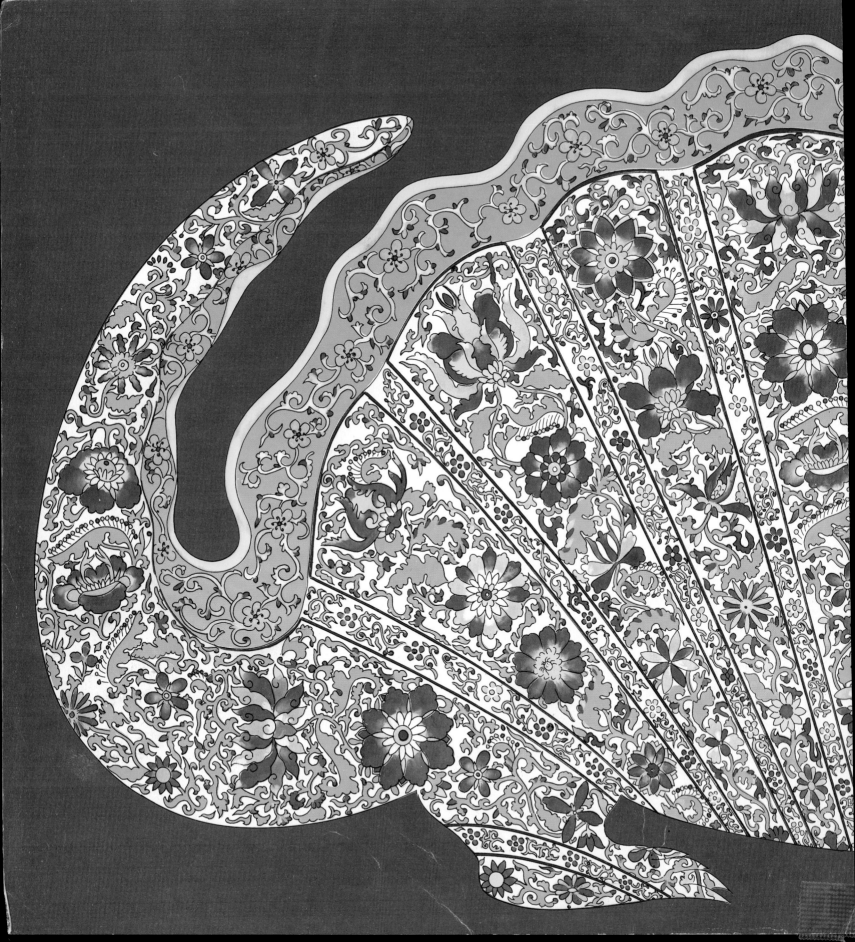

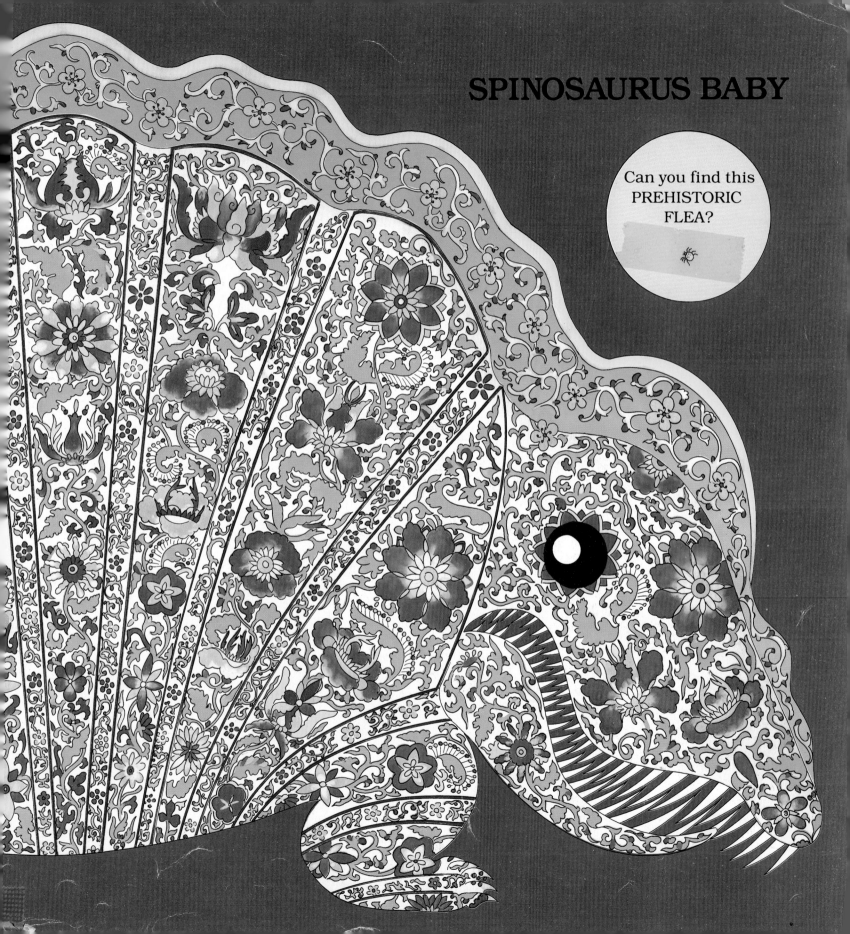

SPINOSAURUS BABY

Can you find this
PREHISTORIC
FLEA?

RHAMPHORYNCHUS

Can you find this
DRAGONFLY?

Can you find this
RHAMPHORYNCHUS?

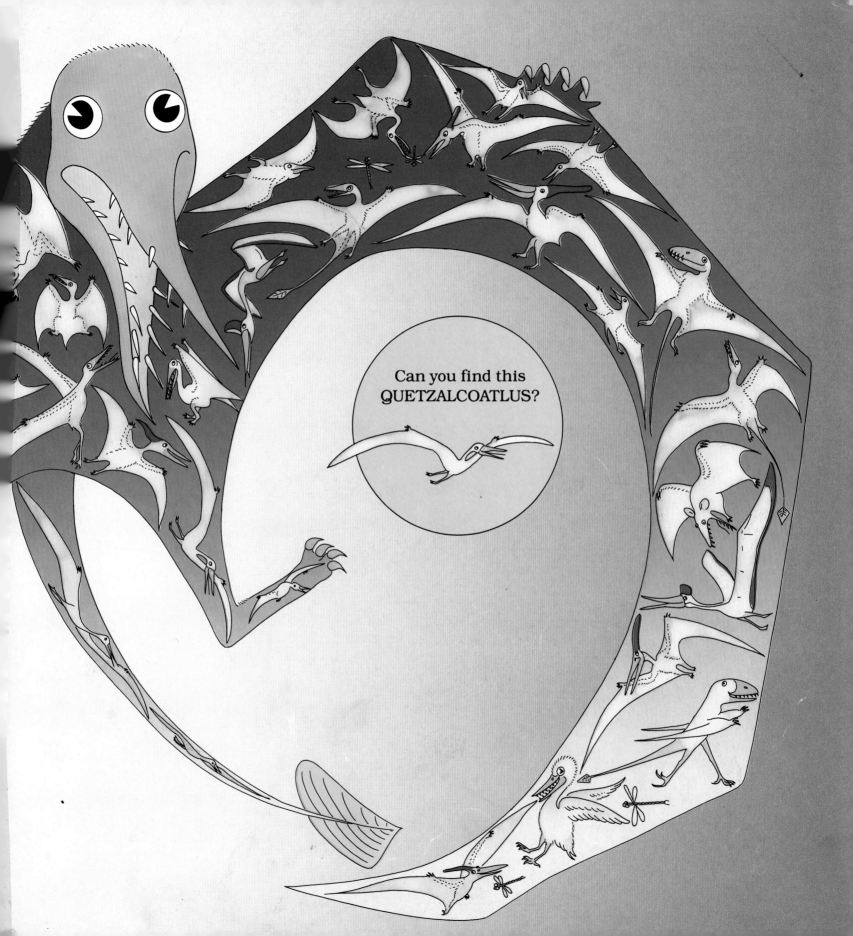

Can you find this
QUETZALCOATLUS?

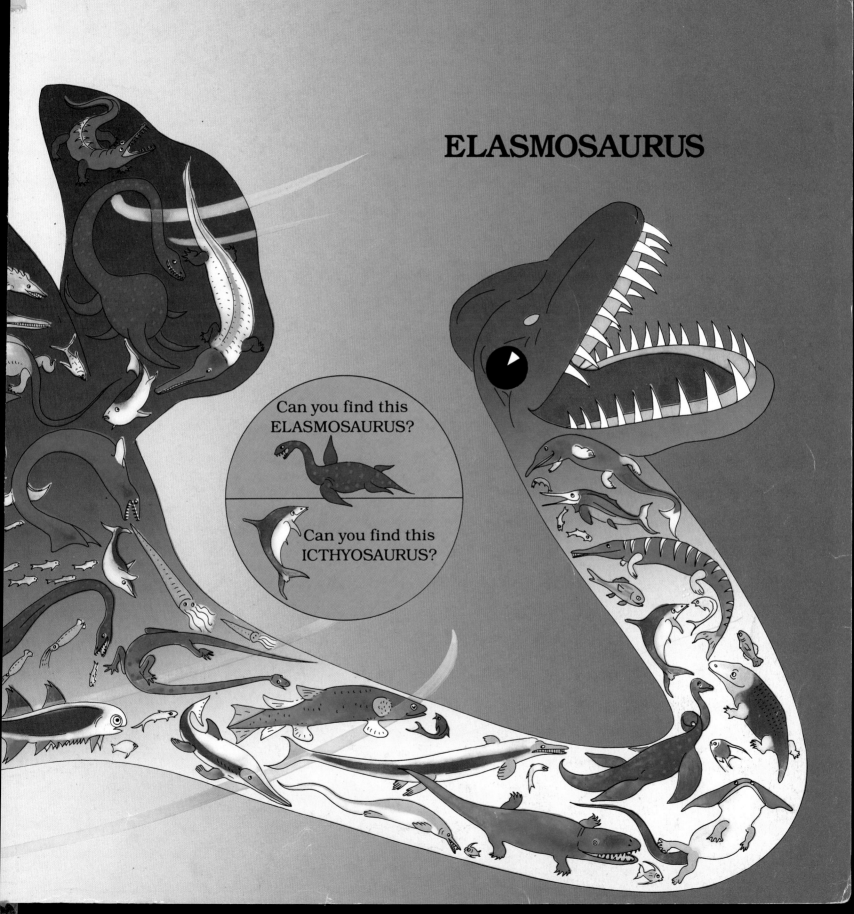

ELASMOSAURUS

Can you find this
ELASMOSAURUS?

Can you find this
ICTHYOSAURUS?

TYRANNOSAURUS

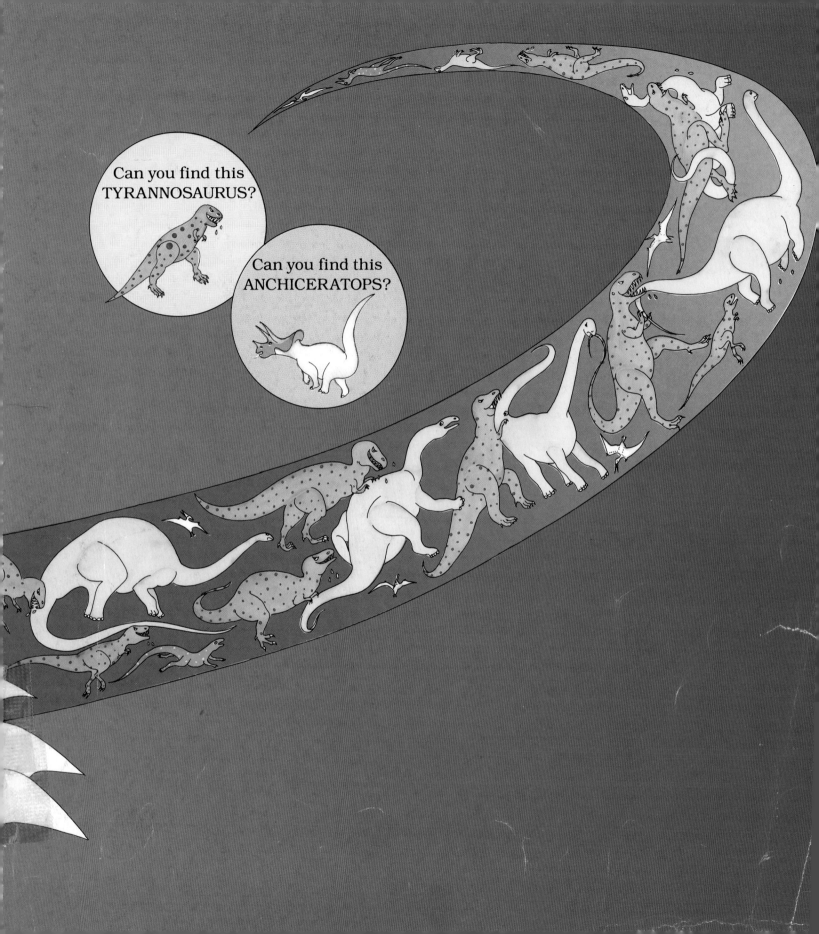

PTERANODON

Can you find this
PTERANODON?

ANKYLOSAURUS

Can you find this
ANKYLOSAURUS?

CHASMOSAURUS

Can you find this
CHASMOSAURUS?

DRYPTOSAURUS

Can you find this
DRYPTOSAURUS?

Can you find this
ELASMOSAURUS?

Can you find this
CORYTHOSAURUS?

Can you find this
PARASAUROLOPHUS?

PARASAUROLOPHUS

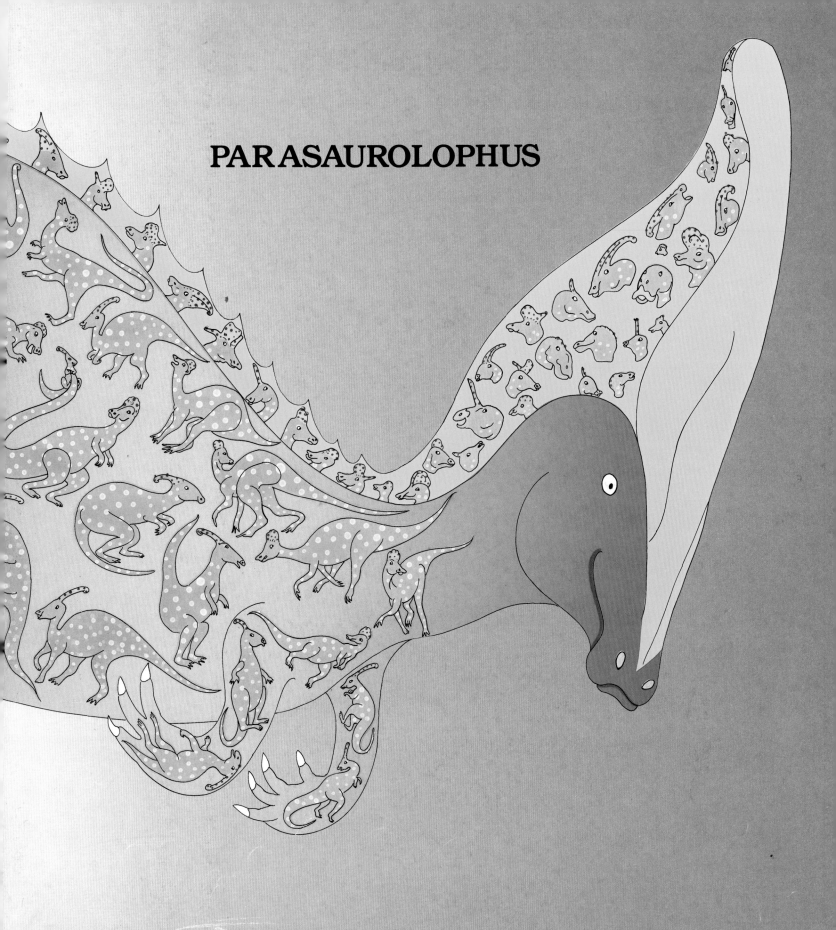

ARCHAEOPTERYX

DEINONYCHUS

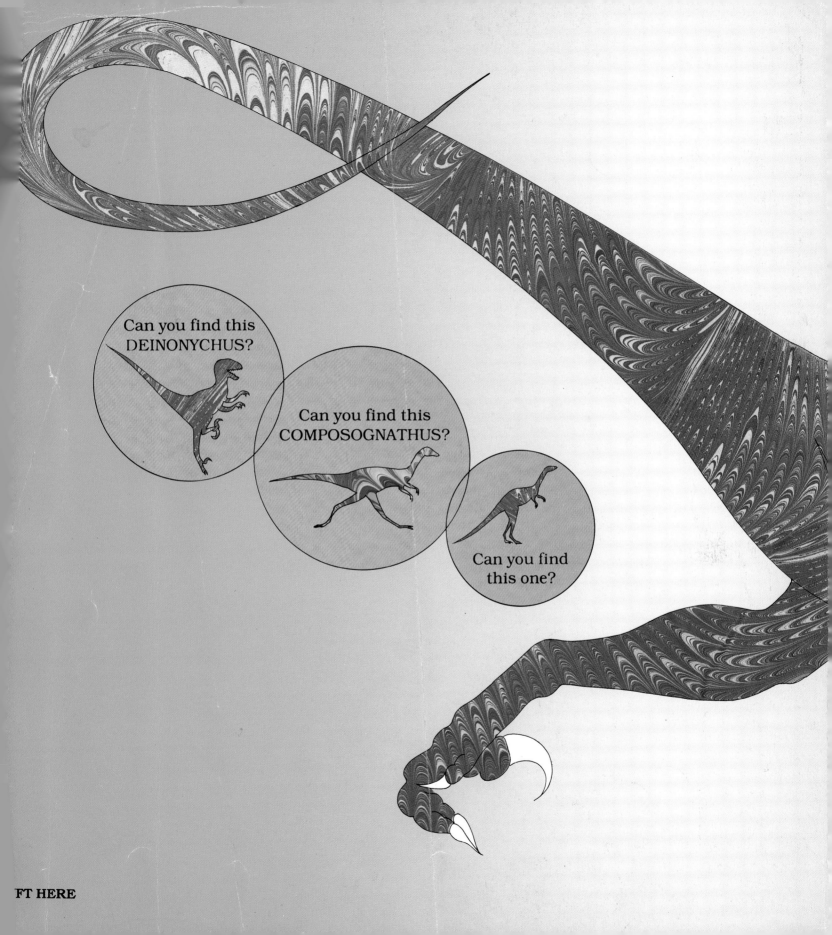

Can you find this
PSITTACOSAURUS?

PSITTACOSAURUS

Can you find this
ARCHAEOPTERYX?

COMPOSOGNATHUS

TRICERATOPS

Can you find this baby
TRICERATOPS?

Can you find this one?

IGUANODON

THERE'S MORE TO THIS PAGE ➔

MAMENCHISAURUS

Can you find this
IGUANODON?

LIFT HERE

PACHYCEPHALOSAURUS

Can you find these
PACHYCEPHALOSAURS?

T HERE

Go back and find this
PACHYCEPHALOSAURUS:

Find this MEGANEURA:

Find this ARCHAEOPTERYX:

Find this TRICERATOPS:

Find this BARYONYX:

Find this BABY IGUANODON:

Find this EDMONTOSAURUS:

Find this MAMENCHISAURUS:

Clue: Now that you have reached this stage,
Look on every *purple* page.

this page.

CLARKE

CLARKE

411   Demi
              Find Demi's
        Dinosaurs

SWAMPSCOTT ELEMENTARY SCHOOL LIBRARIES
        SWAMPSCOTT MASSACHUSETTS